'QUOTE AND UNQUOTE'

'QUOTE AND UNQUOTE'

Edited by Peter and Josie Holtom

Illustrated by Quentin Blake

UNABRIDGED

PAN BOOKS LTD : LONDON

First published 1970 by The Arcadia Press
for the Diners Club of Great Britain
This edition published 1973 by
Pan Books Ltd, 33 Tothill Street, London SW1

ISBN 0 330 23802 7

Made and printed in Great Britain by
Cox & Wyman Ltd, London, Reading and Fakenham

Publisher's Note

✳

The quotes in this book are in no way 'classified'. So many anthologies of quotations have them grouped under headings, perhaps to add weight to their significance, that we decided not to. The order in which the quotes appear in this unusual anthology corresponds approximately to the dates of their original publication in the Diners Club magazine *Signature*.

We hope you will enjoy reading this book as much as we have. To the after-dinner speaker we make no apology for the absence of 'headings'. We are sure in searching for quotes on your favourite subject you will find many others to add to your collection.

Our thanks are due to the Diners Club for their cooperation in the production of the book, and to Quentin Blake for his delightful illustrations – and not least to all those who have contributed to *Signature* such a splendid variety of interesting and often hilarious quotations.

Foreword

from the publisher of Signature

❋

As this interesting little book clearly demonstrates, there are quotations on most subjects under the sun. There are even a few on the subject of words themselves.

The master of them all, Sir Winston Churchill, was of the opinion that 'the short words are the best, and the old words best of all'. William Hazlitt averred that 'words are the only things that last for ever'. Napoleon said 'it is astonishing what power words have over man'.

In 'Quote and Unquote' there are hundreds of pithy, amusing sayings from which you can choose. Some are useful for that after-dinner speech, for the important address to fellow directors or staff, or for the otherwise off-the-cuff reply at an informal social event.

There is another good use too – to be read just because they are entertaining and light-hearted or because you like an anthology which you can pick up and put down when the mood takes you.

The quotations have all appeared in the pages of Signature, the monthly magazine where 'Quote and Unquote' has been a popular feature. I am sure you will enjoy them too. They all have one thing in common. As is the soul of wit, they are brief. We all have our favourite examples of brief but devastating remarks made by the great. My own is the story about the young writer who complained to Oscar Wilde, 'There seems to be a conspiracy of silence about my books. What would you advise me to do?' Quick as lightning, Wilde replied, 'Join it.'

1966

❊

The biggest trouble with success is that its formula is just about the same as that for a nervous break-down. *John Holmes*

❊

As an actress I have always wanted to play Cleo-patra, but I've had to give up the idea now that I'm seventy-five. *Margaret Rutherford*

❊

The biggest mystery to a married man is what a bachelor does with his money. *Alan King*

❊

Prospective buyer to an electronic-brain salesman: '£250,000 is a little steep. Do you have one with a lower IQ?' *S. Lee*

❊

Woman, watching football match in pouring rain, to husband: 'This is probably just another one of my silly questions, but why don't we go home?' *M. Coe*

The man who can smile when things go wrong has probably just thought of someone he can blame it on. *E. Freeman*

❋

Hawaii is the most difficult spot in the world to leave; everywhere else they wave goodbye with their hands. *J. Friday*

❋

It is also possible that blondes prefer gentlemen. *M. Van Doren*

❋

On accepting an award: 'I don't deserve this, but I have arthritis and I don't deserve that either.' *Jack Benny*

❋

The haves and the have-nots can often be traced back to the dids and the did-nots. *Bob Goddard*

❋

Confidence is simply that quiet, assured feeling you have just before you fall flat on your face. *Dr L. Binder*

❋

Women love the simpler things in life – men. *J. Fineger*

Wife to husband: 'One of the trout you were fishing for last weekend phoned and left her number.' *James McLeod*

❉

Pedestrian: a husband who didn't think the family needed two cars. *Bruce Patterson*

❉

Secretary: 'And when I asked him if he wanted the carbon double-spaced too, he really blew his top.' *Tom Ewell*

❉

Girl at cocktail party to wolf: 'All right, Mr Jones, so you can read me like a book – but would you mind not thumbing through the pages?' *Rona Greer*

❉

'I found a way to make my wife drive more carefully. I told her that if she had an accident, the newspapers would print her age!' *Jan Murray*

❉

A youngster, lunching with his mother, told her that his new teacher was 'mean, but fair'. 'How's that?' asked his mother. 'Oh, she's mean to everyone.' *Frank Farre*

❉

Perhaps those suits are called bikinis because they don't cover the girls atoll. *Robert Orben*

I have reached that age in life where it is harder to *find* temptation than it is to resist it. *E. E. Calhoun*

❋

Every time I see the portrait of Whistler's mother, I think of the tot who described her as 'A nice old lady waiting for the repairman to bring back her TV set.' *E. Wilson.*

❋

From a book review: 'It is not a book to be lightly thrown aside. It should be thrown with great force.' *Robert Green*

❋

Groucho Marx, when told he could smoke cigars on the aeroplane if he didn't annoy the lady passengers: 'You mean there's a choice? Then I'll annoy the ladies.' *Thomas April*

❋

The biggest problem you face at this time of year is to convince the kids that you're Father Christmas and your wife that you aren't. *Communication*

❋

Small boy to girl: 'If I sit across from you at the table does that mean I'm the opposite sex?' *Tom H. Miles*

All I'm looking for is a man who is kind and under-standing. Is that too much to ask of a millionaire? *M. Van Doren*

※

Many are saved from sin by being so inept at it. *M. McLaughlin*

※

Frowning psychiatrist to nurse on phone: 'Just say we're terribly busy – NOT "It's a madhouse." ' *Dr L. Binder*

※

A book is a success when people who haven't read it pretend they have. *J. McCarthy*

※

Lady to bank teller: 'I'd like to open a joint ac-count with someone who has plenty of money.' *H. Courtney*

※

Significant sign on a Rolls-Royce: 'This status symbol for sale. Owner unfortunately changing status.' *O. Arnold*

※

There's a new petrol that puts a rabbit in your tank – it's for short hops. *Dr L. Binder*

Any man who says he can see through women is missing a lot. *Groucho Marx*

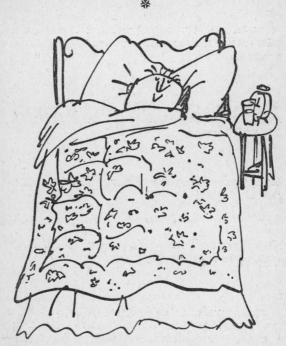

The amount of sleep required by the average person is about five minutes more. *Norris Cool*

Sign on a tiny sports car parked in front of a Birmingham hospital: 'Premature'. *M. Day*

Among the things that money can't buy is what it used to. *William Short*

✸

Girl to escort: 'Stop saying you love to watch the wind and rain in my hair and call a taxi.' *Linda Montwill*

✸

It's not that I really cheat at golf. I play for my health, and a low score makes me feel better. *Robert E. Wilson*

✸

Taxi: vehicle that always seems to dissolve in the rain. *D. Bennett*

✸

Never question your wife's judgement. Look at who she married. *Rona Greer*

✸

There's a wonderful new baby food on the market. It's half orange juice and half garlic. It not only makes the baby healthier, but easier to find in the dark. *John Batchelder*

✸

The reason it takes a woman longer to dress is because she has to slow down on the curves. *Morey Amsterdam/contributed by Gordon Irving*

The world is full of checks and balances. Just when you get to the point where menu prices don't matter, calories do. *Phil Harris*

⁂

One teacher to another: 'Not only is he the worst-behaved child in school, but he also has a perfect attendance record.' *National Observer*

⁂

No man is really old until his mother stops worrying about him. *William Ryan*

⁂

The Chairman of the Board is the man who can take as long as he wants to make a snap decision. *H. Priday*

⁂

Notice in a Brighton hotel: 'Our waiters are your good friends. Please do not insult them by tipping.' A few feet away from the notice one of the waiters has placed a box marked 'Insults'. *Evening Standard*

⁂

If your wife wants to drive, don't stand in her way. *E. Craig*

A father says his teen-age son took an aptitude test for a job and was found to be best suited for retirement. *Deane Binder*

❋

There was the woman who told her husband, 'Be an angel and let me drive.' He did and he is. *Bob Goddard*

❋

For years women have said they haven't a thing to wear. Well, this year they're wearing it. *Robert Orben*

❋

Little girl, rebelliously practising the piano, to father: 'Another way for me to be popular when I grow up is for you to be rich.' *E. Brown*

❋

Small son to father: 'Why should lemonade spoil my dinner and martinis give you an appetite?' *Frances Benson*

1967

❋

English laws punish vice; the Chinese laws do more, they reward virtue. *Contributed by I. Burman*

❋

My wife has been driving for two months and she isn't joking when she comes home and says, 'Guess who I ran into today?' *Bob Goddard*

❋

There's often a family tie between father and son, but the son is usually wearing it. *Anna Herbert*

❋

The world is full of willing people; some willing to work, the rest willing to let them. *Robert Frost/contributed by Arthur J. Lewis, MP*

❋

A doorman is a genius who can open the door of your car with one hand, help you in with the other, and still have one left for the tip. *Dorothy Kilgallen/contributed by Gordon Irving*

Some people play golf religiously – every Sunday. *Derek Stevens*

✳

There's a story on the children's page of a trade union journal which begins: 'Once upon a time and a half . . .' *Communication*

✳

The drawback in setting a good example for your children is that it takes all the fun out of your own middle age. *'600' Magazine/contributed by E. Bryant*

✳

Prophesying is difficult, especially where the future is concerned. *Robert Storm-Petersen/contributed by John Drinkall*

✳

Picking up a Dr Barnardo's collection envelope with the picture of a child on the front, four-year-old child runs out to his mother, who is planting seeds in the garden, crying: 'Look Mummy, seeds for growing babies!' *Contributed by Joan Waltham.*

✳

I love criticism, just so long as it's unqualified praise. *Noel Coward/contributed by T. Launer*

✳

Men fall into three classes – the handsome, the intelligent, and the majority. *Contributed by F. G. Benson*

People today are chiefly concerned with the higher things in life – like prices. *Rona Greer*

❋

Punctuality is something that if you have, there's often no one around to share it with you. *Hylda Baker/contributed by George Bartram*

❋

There is no economy in going to bed early to save candles if the result is twins. *Chinese proverb/contributed by F. W. Matthews*

❋

Why shouldn't I call my wife an angel? She's always up in the air about something, always harping on my faults and never has an earthly thing to wear. *R. Bauman*

❋

We are constantly amazed at these young things with their fancy hairdos and skintight pants. And the girls are even worse. *Wall Street Journal*

❋

A former Speaker, House of Commons: 'Let us never forget that many a brave heart beats beneath the kilt of the Cameron Highlander.' *Arthur J. Lewis, MP*

'I am very fond of children; especially girl children of about 16 or 17 years old.' *W. C. Fields/contributed by J. F. Baron*

※

In this world there are the righteous and unrighteous. It is the righteous who decide who are the unrighteous. *Contributed by S. C. Brittle*

※

Woman showing dented car to garage mechanic: 'The bumper's been acting up again!' *Frances Goldman*

※

If, at the end of two or three minutes you haven't struck oil, give up boring. *James Russel Lowell/contributed by J. Drinkall*

※

Many a man who marries a wisp of a girl is astonished at the will o' the wisp. *Thomas April*

※

When a man doesn't care tuppence what he says, you generally find nobody else does either. *Contributed by Mrs J. H. Pollard*

※

'Since I told the Chairman where he got off,' writes a member, 'he's a different person. And I'm with a different company.' *Communication*

A career woman is a woman who goes out and earns a man's salary instead of staying at home and taking it away from him. *Contributed by S. Miller*

※

Misers are no fun to live with, but as ancestors they're great. *Contributed by G. W. Stephenson*

※

Blessed is the man who has nothing to say and cannot be persuaded to say it. *Contributed by F. G. Benson*

※

Man receiving award at special dinner: 'My wife deserves credit for my success. Her steady doubt and ridicule gave me the necessary incentive to win.' *American Legion Magazine*

※

Worry is the interest paid on trouble before it is due. *Dr W. R. Inge/contributed by F. W. Matthews*

※

Overheard at retirement presentation: 'And I shall always recall my service here as forty years of tedium relieved by tea breaks.' *Communication*

An optimist is a man who hasn't had much experience. *Don Marquis/contributed by M. V. Hynes*

❋

André Simon, the 90-year-old founder of the Wine and Food Society, was asked at a recent function whether he ever drank water. 'Rarely,' he replied. 'You see I have an iron constitution and I do not want it to rust.' *Contributed by Rupert Denny*

❋

If you try, you might. If you don't you won't. *Wilfred Pickles/contributed by P. G. Farmer*

❋

History is always repeating itself, but each time the price goes up. *Contributed by S. Miller*

❋

The best training for bachelorhood is marriage. *Contributed by Peter Evans*

❋

A man celebrates his birthday by taking a day off. A woman takes a year off. *Morey Amsterdam/contributed by Gordon Irving*

❋

You're getting old when the girl you smile at thinks you're one of her father's friends. *Arthur Murray*

To get maximum attention, it's hard to beat a good, big mistake. *Hanover Gazette*

✳

The first thing that strikes a visitor to Paris is a taxi. *V. L. Guffey*

✳

Just because nobody disagrees with you does not necessarily mean you are brilliant – maybe you're the boss. *John Holmes*

✳

Wife, pointing to her husband stretched out in the hammock, explains to her friend: 'Fred's hobby is letting birds watch him.' *John Marshall*

Never trust to memory what you can put down in writing. Never put down in writing what can be used in evidence against you. *P. J. Kelsey*

❋

Mother of small boy to psychiatrist: 'Well, I don't know whether he feels insecure, but everybody else in the neighbourhood certainly does.' *V. L. Guffey*

❋

In Africa, the natives have the custom of beating the ground with clubs and uttering blood-curdling yells. Anthropologists call this a form of primitive self-expression. However, in Britain, we have another name for it – golf. *F. C. Francis*

❋

It must be discouraging to a sensible girl when she observes the way sensible men smile at silly girls. *Simon Jones*

❋

Of course I believe in luck. How otherwise do you explain the success of the people you detest? *Jean Cocteau*

❋

My children are at the perfect age – too old to cry at night and too young to borrow my car. *Walter Slezak*

❋

Whenever I meet a man who would make a good husband, he is. *Susan Oliver*

Before television, nobody even knew what a headache looked like. *D. Fields*

❊

Middle-age is when the narrow waist and the broad mind begin to change places. *Patricia Moody*

❊

A bachelor is a man who only has to make one breakfast before he goes to work. *Anna Herbert*

❊

Marriage is a process by which a man finds out the sort of husband his wife thinks she should have had. *Contributed by Angela Robinson*

❊

I remember my class-mates – cauliflower ears, broken noses, split lips – and the boys were just as bad! *Jimmy Tarbuck/contributed by J. Cooke*

❊

You can't be sure of anything these days. Just think of all the mothers who, 20 years ago, had their daughters vaccinated in places they thought wouldn't show. *V. L. Guffey*

❊

It is reassuring to note that many a pillar of wisdom ends up as a column in the *News of the World*. *Contributed by J. E. Perry*

I'm not really heavy – I'm just short for my weight. I should actually be about 8 feet 6 inches. *Jackie Gleason*

✳

Mixed emotions is being middle-aged and suddenly realizing you'll never be a has-been. *Francis O. Walsh*

✳

It's no good having a spark of genius if you suffer from ignition trouble. *Communication*

✳

One woman to another: 'I won't go into details – I've already told you more than I heard myself.' *Henry Martin*

✳

One of the Freedoms of the English is freedom from culture. *Lord Goodman/contributed by W. John Merrick*

✳

Experience tells us that a thing of beauty is a great expense. *Contributed by Leslie Page*

✳

She is 19 going on 20 and he is 50 going on pep pills. *James Harris*

A bee's sting is only one-thirty-second of an inch long. The other five inches is imagination. *Derek Marshall*

✳

Nurse to impatient expectant father: 'Just because you have been kept waiting doesn't necessarily mean that the baby will be a girl!' *Henry Leabo*

✳

I know a chap with a very serious drinking problem – he has no money for drinks. *Thomas April*

✳

Ego is when a man, sitting in a crowded bus, flirts with a woman who is standing. *Clyde Melton*

✳

Handicapped golfer: one who is playing with the boss. *S. Lee*

✳

The early bird catches less sleep. *Contributed by L. Brophy*

Let us be thankful for the fools; but for them the rest of us could not succeed. *Contributed by E. Franklin*

❋

It is better to be a 'drunk' than an 'alcoholic'. A drunk doesn't have to attend all those damn meetings. *Contributed by Arthur J. Lewis, MP*

❋

They say that if you don't smoke, don't drink, and don't go out with women you live longer. Actually it only seems longer. *Mark Twain/contributed by J. G. Miller*

Usefulness is the rent we pay for our room on this
earth – many of us are heavily in debt. *Contributed
by F. W. Garrard*

✻

Company Secretary: 'I cannot approve this expense account, Brown, but we'd like to buy the
fiction rights to it.' *Contributed by E. Bryant*

✻

A honeymoon is a holiday that a man takes before
starting work for a new boss. *Contributed by John
Rhodes*

✻

Today's teenagers can be described in one word:
'Fastidious' – the girls are fast, and the boys are
'hideous'. *Contributed by F. A. Cullis*

✻

He that will not reason is a bigot; he that cannot
reason is a fool; and he that dares not reason is a
slave. *Sir W. Drummond/contributed by W. Hen-
riques*

✻

When Henry Ford was asked for the recipe for a
long and happy marriage, he replied, 'Always stick
to the same model.' *Contributed by A. M.
Ponder*

Money can't buy friends but it gets you a better class of enemy. *Contributed by A. Naul*

＊

The more I see of the average parent the more I respect the average boy. *Sir John Laird McClure/ contributed by S. W. Smyth*

＊

I spent a year in that town one Sunday. *Fred Allen/contributed by C. Hemming*

＊

Past experiences make future confidences. *Contributed by J. P. Colliss*

＊

All too often the life of the party is the death of conversation. *Contributed by G. B. O'Boyce*

＊

Epitaph on the tombstone of the very superior Head Waiter: 'God caught his eye at last.' *Contributed by K. S. Tollit*

＊

Irate taxi driver to passenger: 'There'll be no charge, lady. You did most of the driving.' *N. Havens*

After you've heard two eye-witness accounts of a car accident, you begin to wonder about history. *Rona Greer*

❋

A friend tells me his wife keeps her figure by eating everything she wants. 'Otherwise,' he said, 'how could she stay at 16 stone?' *B. Bacherach*

❋

Husband looking over bills, to wife: 'Well, we're at the bridge we were going to cross when we came to it!' *Patricia Moody*

❋

Doctor giving prescription to patient: 'Let me know if this stuff works. I'm having the same trouble myself.' *James Sherman*

❋

Between the golden years of youth and the golden years of retirement come those nickel-plated years when you do all the work. *Bill Vaughan*

❋

There ought to be a better way to start the day than by getting up in the morning. *Robert E. Wilson*

❋

If you've been watching the TV commercials, you get the impression that Venus de Milo must have used too harsh a detergent. *Patricia Moody*

Sign in a laundry window: 'We do not tear your clothes by machine — we do it carefully by hand.'
Fay Ceder

＊

A youthful figure is something you get when you ask a woman her age. *Contributed by P. H. Buckley*

＊

My wife happens to be very big in karate circles. You know those fellows who can break three boards with one chop? Who do you think cooks the chop?
Robert Orben

＊

Just when we thought we knew all there is to know about sex, we went to see a Swedish film. Now we're starting all over again. *H. Boyle*

＊

Behind every successful man is an astonished wife.
B. W. Olver

＊

On his tenth anniversary, a band leader who had played at over 2,000 dances was asked, 'What have you had the most requests for?' 'Where's the men's room?' answered the maestro. *Bill Thorpe*

It is better to keep your mouth shut and be thought a fool than to open it and remove all doubt. *Contributed by D. Bass*

❋

The measure of a man's real character is what he would do if he knew he would never be found out. *Contributed by G. McGreevy*

❋

Two expectant mothers seated in a bus were over-heard discussing doctors in general, when one finally commented in a positive tone: 'Well, at least in our case they can't say "it's all in your mind".' *D. Rose*

❋

A closed mouth gathers no foot. *Robert E. Wilson*

❋

The best of spontaneous remarks requires very careful rehearsals. *Contributed by H. P. Hartley*

❋

'You heckled me ten years ago – I don't remember your face but I recognize the suit you're wearing.' *Contributed by Sam Lomberg*

❋

Some people are still willing to do an honest day's work, but they want a week's pay for it. *Andrew Preston*

The trouble with my golf game is that I stand too close to the ball after I've hit it. *Jack Benny*

✷

She's rather like Venus de Milo — beautiful, but not all there. *Contributed by W. H. Boorne*

✷

Perhaps it's only coincidence, but man's best friend can't talk. *Jimmy Cannon*

✷

'Money is not everything,' as the American millionaire said to his son. 'A man with nine million dollars can be just as happy as the man with ten million.' *Contributed by Henry Button*

✷

Nowadays when your ship comes in the Inland Revenue sees it is safely docked. *Contributed by Leslie Page*

✷

If all else fails, give up. *S. Frederick*

✷

It is always best not to tell people your troubles. Half of them are not interested, and the other half are glad you're getting what's coming to you. *AMA News*

✷

My car is so small I have to pay my parking fines in the Juvenile Court. *Derek Holmes*

I've reached the most disappointing time of my life – my wife now trusts me. *James Kayakos*

✳

My doctor advised me to give up those intimate little dinners for two – unless I had one other person eating with me. *John Marshall*

✳

Another thing that makes man unique is that he is the only living thing that needs advice on how to grow old. *J. M. Loughlin*

✳

Any child who gets raised by the book must be a first edition. *D. S. Mowatt*

✳

A bachelor is a man who never Mrs anybody. *T. Stone*

I seem to be growing old alone. My wife hasn't had a birthday for six years. *Martin White*

✻

The latest thing in clothes is usually the woman you're waiting for. *John Rose*

✻

Marriage is a mutual admiration society where one person is always in the right and the other one is the husband. *W. Grant*

✻

After dinner speaking is an occupation monopolized by men – women can't wait that long. *Contributed by S. Miller*

✻

Inscription on the tombstone of a notorious hypochondriac: 'See!' *Michael Jones*

✻

Economists are still trying to work out why the girl with the least principle draws the most interest. *G. Black*

✻

Happiness is watching a snow-plough cover a police car. *J. Davidson*

In the old days, if you wanted to know if a girl had knock-knees you had to listen. *Vic Damone*

❋

Nothing is as ancient as progress. *Japanese proverb/contributed by Barry Hertzog*

❋

Worry never robs tomorrow of its sorrow. It only saps today of its strength. *Contributed by E. Franklin*

❋

Most children enjoy seeing flowers come up – mostly by the roots. *Contributed by Leslie Page*

Some people have little to say, but you have to listen a long time to find out. *Contributed by W. H. Boorne*

❊

Television is a device that enables people who haven't anything to do to watch people who can't do anything. *Fred Allen/contributed by Gordon Irving*

❊

'My advice, sir,' said the mechanic to the car owner, 'is that you keep the oil and change the car.' *A. Dickey*

❊

How sweet it is to hear one's own convictions from a stranger's mouth. *Goethe/contributed by Malcolm Line*

❊

Those who want much are always much in need. *Horace/contributed by G. Alterman*

❊

Overheard at a party: 'No, Joe has never married — he's just a self-made mouse.' *Frances Benson*

❊

By the time a man finds greener pastures, he can't climb the fence. *Ernest Boone*

I have just worked out why blondes have more fun.
You can find them in the dark. *Robert Orben*

❋

As is the case with a light bulb, the man who is
always switched on is the first to burn out. *Wall
Street Journal*

❋

Middle age is that time of life when you can feel
bad in the morning without having fun the night
before. *M. Hamilton*

❋

Heredity is what makes the mother and father of
teenagers wonder a little about each other. *G. L.
Hull*

❋

'I was told not to shoot until I saw the whites of
their thighs.' *Cameraman working on X certificate
film/contributed by Leslie Page*

❋

I have a suspicion that when one astronaut is being
encouraged to walk into space by another astronaut, the motivation is the .45 held by the other
astronaut. *Simon Day*

Husband scolding wife: 'Where's the dust on this table? I had a 'phone number written on it!' *James Tod*

1968

A prejudiced person is one who doesn't believe in the same things as we do. *Contributed by N. Strucken*

A marriage is an alliance between a man who cannot sleep with the window open and a woman who cannot sleep with the window shut. *Contributed by F. C. Pyke*

There are only two things a child will share willingly – communicable diseases and his mother's age. *Dr Benjamin Spock*

Notice in a café window: Don't stand outside and look miserable, come inside and be fed up. *Contributed by John L. Luckie*

Personnel manager to shapely blonde: 'You're just the type we're looking for – we've decided to let some of our computers go.' *James Brown*

Worry is like a rocking chair, keeps you going but gets you nowhere. *Contributed by V. A. Sharp*

Overheard in a London restaurant: 'Of course, it's the lighting that is subdued here, not the prices.' *T. J. Timblick*

※

I have discontinued long speeches on account of my throat. Several people have threatened to cut it. *Contributed by Arthur J. Lewis, MP*

※

I have stopped arguing with my teenage son about borrowing the car. Now, whenever I want it, I take it. *G. E. Meyer*

※

A Texan walked into a motor-car dealer's and said to the salesman: 'I'd like to send my wife a get-well car.' *Morey Amsterdam/contributed by Gordon Irving*

※

One often finds that the best thing about distant relations is the distance. *Contributed by W. Stanley James*

※

One reason that history repeats itself is that so many people were not listening the first time. *Margaret Hussey*

The football season is the only time of the year when a man can walk down the street with a blonde on one arm and a blanket on the other without encountering raised eyebrows. *M. H. Beuchat*

❋

Prosperity will be here again when men's trousers begin to bag at the pocket and not at the knees. *The Speakers Desk Book/contributed by W. G. Comer*

❋

Diner to waiter: 'Are you the waiter I placed my order with? I was expecting an older man.' *Contributed by John L. James*

❋

By the time a man has money to burn, the fire has gone out. *Contributed by L. Winthrop*

❋

Statistics are like a bikini . . . what they reveal may be interesting, but what they conceal is fascinating. *Contributed by David Colyer*

❋

Those who warn of a population explosion picture a world with too many people and not enough food – like the average cocktail party. *Bill Vaughan*

What I admire about Columbus is not his having discovered a new world, but his having gone to search for it on the faith of an opinion. *Frances Benson*

❋

Don't drive with one arm round your girl friend. Let her drive, and then you can use two arms. *Contributed by Peter Mocsari*

❋

A bachelor is a chap who fails to embrace his opportunities. *Contributed by W. Lawrence*

❋

Ever notice that a girl with bad legs never sees a mouse? *Ernest Miller*

❋

If Moses had been a committee, the Israelites would still be in Egypt. *J. B. Hughes/contributed by F. W. Matthews*

❋

Desperation is a man who shaves before weighing himself on the bathroom scales. *Robert E. Dorsey.*

❋

Despite the squeeze, a penny for many people's thoughts *is* still a fair price. *Dickie Henderson/contributed by George Bartram*

A low neckline is something you can look down upon and approve of at the same time. *Contributed by P. H. Buckley*

❉

It isn't doing the job that takes the time, it's the starting and the finishing of it. *Contributed by G. V. Rickards*

Home is heaven and orgies are vile, but you need an orgy once in a while. *Ogden Nash/contributed by E. Nadler*

❋

Ability is a poor man's wealth. *Matthew Wren*

❋

Appetizers are little things you keep eating until you lose your appetite. *Good Housekeeping*

❋

You come into the world with nothing – anything you get after that is sheer profit. *Tommy Steele/contributed by L. Winthrop*

Drunk man in railway carriage to woman opposite: 'Madam, you are very ugly.' She replied, 'You are very drunk.' This exchange of courtesies continued until the woman was getting out. The man shouted after her, 'Madam, tomorrow I shall be sober but you will still be ugly.' *Contributed by Eugen Spier*

❄

Don't drive as though you have only one day to live ... you could be right. *Contributed by W. G. Comer*

❄

It's easy to recognize a home owner. He's always coming out of a hardware shop. *Andrew Johnson*

❄

All generalizations are dangerous, even this one. *Alexandre Dumas*

❄

A politician is a man who is interested in wordy causes. *Evelyn Chase*

❄

Income is something you cannot live without or within. *Contributed by Leslie Page*

❄

Sign at street crossing: 'Watch out for school children, especially if they are driving cars.' *M. H. Beuchat*

Sign on a golf course: 'Members will please refrain from picking up lost golf balls until they have stopped rolling.' *Golf News*

❋

I have often wanted to drown my troubles, but I can't get my wife to go swimming. *J. Carter*

❋

The honeymoon is over when he stops helping her with the dishes and does them himself. *Contributed by W. G. Comer*

❋

Personnel manager explaining regulations to the new secretary: 'Or if you prefer, you may elect to skip coffee break and retire three years earlier.' *C. Neville*

❋

We cannot blame Wilson for everything that is wrong with Britain today; no one man could do all the damage that he has done. *Glyn Griffiths/ contributed by Anna M. Kirwan*

❋

My insurance policy was like a bikini, minimum cover and maximum risk. *Contributed by F. J. Ball*

A sadist is a doctor who keeps his stethoscope in the refrigerator. *Adam Di Petto*

✳

Acquaintance: a person whom we know well enough to borrow from but not well enough to lend to. *Ambrose Bierce*

✳

If you want to sacrifice the admiration of many men for the criticism of one – go ahead, get married. *A. Gibbs*

Women have a keen sense of humour. The more you humour them the better they like it. *Contributed by R. G. Hunt*

❀

Confidence is a feeling you have before you really understand the problem. *A. Brown*

❀

Don't take life too seriously because you'll never get out of it alive. *Contributed by V. A. Sharp*

❀

Everything has got a moral if you can only find it. *Lewis Carroll*

❀

The religion of one age is the literary entertainment of the next. *R. W. Emerson*

❀

A man is not old until regrets take the place of dreams. *Contributed by Frances August*

❀

One thing about the speed of light – it gets here far too early in the morning. *James Sherman*

'Do you say your prayers before you eat?'
  'No, my mum is a good cook.' *Contributed by Andrew Cross*

✳

Seen on the office notice board — 'Any young executive having no secretary of his own is permitted to take advantage of the girls in the typing pool.' *Contributed by F. C. Pyke*

✳

Intuition is what enables a woman to put two and two together and come up with an answer that suits her. *B. Johns*

✳

The trouble is you're only young once; after that you have to think up a good excuse for what you've done. *Contributed by Patricia Warman*

✳

I have a terrible conscience — it doesn't keep me from doing things; it just keeps me from enjoying them. *New York Journal*

✳

Parents used to strike children to discipline them; now it is usually in self-defence. *F. W. Jones*

One humiliating thing about science is that it is gradually filling our homes and offices with appliances cleverer than we are. *Contributed by R. G. Hunt*

✳

Intuition is what makes a woman recognize a mistake when she makes it a second time. *Contributed by S. Miller*

✳

The hardest part of telling young people the facts of life is finding something that they don't already know. *M. H. Beuchat*

✳

Perseverance comes from a strong will: obstinacy from a strong won't. *H. Young*

✳

Nowadays a woman's first grey hair is usually her last one. *G. E. Meyer*

✳

Racial prejudice – pigment of the imagination. *Campost/contributed by M. Ward*

✳

Road maps tell the motorist everything he wants to know, except how to fold them up again. *John Bishop*

Sign in a travel bureau: 'Go Away'. *J. Schaus*

❄

Some minds are like concrete: all mixed up and permanently set. *J. Arthur Vennon*

❄

A good secretary is expected to look like a girl, think like a man, act like a lady and work like a dog. *Nan Hampton*

❄

Definition of a small town: a place in which there is no place to go that you shouldn't. *Edward Reis.*

❄

An alarm clock is a mechanism that is used to scare the daylights into you. *Norris Cool*

❄

A yawn is nature's way of letting married men open their mouths. *Frances Benson*

❄

I was teacher's pet. She kept me in a cage at the back of the class. *Ken Dodd/contributed by George Bartram*

A survey shows that the nation's top executives spend 80 per cent of their time talking. Oddly enough, it is the same percentage that junior executives spend listening. *Patricia Moody*

❀

Applicants for places at University are now being asked if they intend to concentrate on tests or protests. *John Cooper*

❀

It isn't the number of men in your life that counts — it's the *life* in your men. *Mae West/contributed by L. Winthrop*

❀

Entravagance — what a man buys that is no use to his wife. *Contributed by Leslie Page*

❀

I believe in omens — for instance, when I'm on an ocean liner and I see the Captain rowing away in a lifeboat, I worry. *M. Norman*

❀

A bargain — something you cannot possibly use at a price you cannot possibly resist. *Campost/contributed by A. Ward*

An osteopath is a man who works his finger to your bone. *Contributed by R. G. Hunt*

❋

If you would know the value of money, go try to borrow some. *Benjamin Franklin/contributed by G. J. McGreeny*

❋

He is a member of the effluent society. Stinking rich. *Contributed by Barry Phelps*

❋

That money talks I will agree, it always says 'good-bye' to me. *Sir Edmond Stockdale/contributed by F. J. Bergin*

❋

The trouble with sleep is the going to and the coming from. *B. Clyde*

❋

Monkeys are superior to men – when a monkey looks into a mirror, he sees a monkey. *Chazal*

❋

There are no dangerous women, only susceptible men. *Contributed by P. B. D. Bunyan*

Even if man could understand women he still wouldn't believe it. *A. Brown*

❋

A reception clerk at New York Airport picked up the phone. 'How long does it take to fly to New Orleans?' asked the caller.

'Just a minute,' replied the clerk, reaching for the flight schedule.

'Thanks a lot,' said the caller and rang off. *Contributed by A. S. Subramaniam*

❋

Laws are like cobwebs, which may catch small flies, but let wasps and hornets break through. *Swift*

❋

The Bible tells us to love our neighbours and also love our enemies; probably because they are the same people. *G. K. Chesterton/contributed by Victor Grant*

❋

Definition of a nudist camp – place where nothing goes on. *Leo Aikman/contributed by L. I. Smith*

❋

Kissing is a pleasant way of proving two heads are better than one. *W. O. Mann*

No man can sink so low that a woman or a dog won't love him. *Contributed by P. J. Lane*

❋

Valour is to travel on an ocean liner without tipping. Discretion means to come back on a different ship. *Patricia Moody*

❋

A story is current in the Temple that when Mr Justice Eve took silk the usual notification of his intention was sent to the seniors, and from one of them he received the following reply:
'My dear Eve, whether you wear silk or a fig-leaf, I do not care. Adam.'
Contributed by A. S. Subramaniam

❋

The first mini-skirts: Eve's leaves. *M. H. Beuchat*

❋

The secret of happiness is not to do what you like to do, but to like to do what you have to do. *King George/contributed by Graham Spencer*

Patience – a minor form of despair disguised as a virtue. *Ambrose Bierce*

✳

Perhaps the best thing about the future is that it only comes one day at a time. *Dean Acheson*

✳

Definition of a marriage licence is a kind of hunting permit that limits your take to one dear. *F. C. Francis*

✳

After winning an argument with his wife, the wisest thing a man can do is to apologize. *Danny Kaye*

✳

Overheard: the best substitute for experience is being 17 years old. *H. K. McMullen*

✳

Youth – the first 50 years of your life, the first 20 of anyone else's. *Contributed by S. Miller*

✳

Agreeable advice is seldom useful advice. *Massilon*

A luxury becomes a necessity when the neighbours have it. *Contributed by Angela Robinson*

✻

Wild horses couldn't drag a secret out of most women. Unfortunately, they seldom have lunch with wild horses. *Ivern Boyet*

✻

About the only way a woman can get domestic help nowadays is to marry it. *Anna Herbert*

✻

Old age isn't so bad, when you consider the alternative. *Contributed by W. H. Boorne*

✻

He knows little who will tell his wife all he knows. *T. Fuller*

✻

A woman asked for a drinking bowl for her dog. The assistant asked if she wanted it with the inscription. 'For the dog'. 'It really doesn't matter,' she replied. 'My husband never drinks water and the dog can't read.' *Bryan Palmer*

✻

It's not true that men seldom make passes at girls who wear glasses; it's the frame that counts. *Bill Wilson*

People who say they sleep like a baby usually don't have one. *Contributed by R. G. Hunt*

❋

There's only one difference between learning to drive a car and learning to play golf. When you learn to play golf, you don't hit anything. *John Graham*

❋

Youth is fleeting – particularly at the age of fifty. *Pierre Daninds*

❋

Although there exists many thousands of subjects for elegant conversation, there are persons who cannot meet a cripple without talking about feet. *Ernest Bramah/contributed by Frances Gallagher*

❋

A convincing talker is the man who keeps both hands in his pockets while describing the one that got away. *Contributed by G. M. O'Boyce*

❋

A bachelor is like a new detergent, works fast and leaves no ring. *Terry Canterbury*

❋

There is really only one thing wrong with the younger generation – a lot of us don't belong to it any more. *Contributed by S. Miller*

Pleasure's a sin, and sometimes sin's a pleasure.
Lord Byron

❋

There seem nowadays to be two sources of literary inspiration – fullness of mind and emptiness of pocket. *Lowell*

❋

Automation hasn't cut out red tape. It merely perforates it. *James Harris*

❋

Men don't marry women on £15 a week any more – the girl must be making twice that. *Rona Greer*

❋

Disapproving grandmother: 'In my day, if a girl didn't have anything to wear she stayed at home.' *John Conway*

❋

The cigarette warnings have made people nervous. I heard of one bank robber who passed a note to a teller which read: 'Give me all your money or I'll blow smoke in your face.' *Ray Fire*

❋

There is no love sincerer than the love of food. *George Bernard Shaw*

A high dignitary of the church, flying 30,000 feet above the Atlantic, was asked by the stewardess if he would care for a whisky and soda. The churchman hesitated for a moment and then said, 'I think not. We're a little too close to Headquarters.' *Contributed by Leslie Page*

A diplomat is a man who always remembers a woman's birthday but never remembers her age. *R. Frost*

Flattery won't hurt if you don't swallow it. *Hubbard*

It is impossible to enjoy idling thoroughly unless one has plenty of work to do. *Jerome K. Jerome*

People who throw kisses are hopelessly lazy. *Bob Hope/contributed by Dewi Lewis*

The problem of taxation is quite simple. You can shear a sheep repeatedly but can skin it only once. *H. Post*

A monopolist is a person who keeps an elbow on each arm of a cinema seat. *M. C. Bell*

❋

An inferiority complex would be a blessing, if only the right people had it. *Alan Reed*

❋

Resolutions are like eels – easy to catch but hard to hang on to. *Alexandre Dumas/contributed by Dewi Lewis*

❋

An executive usually follows his work schedule to a tee. *M. H. Beuchat*

❋

When the wife brings home information from the Golf Club, it's gossip, but when the husband does likewise, it's news! *Contributed by J. E. Marsh*

❋

Middle age is not the beginning of the end, but the end of the beginning. *L. J. Tizard*

❋

Psychologist – a man who, when a beautiful girl enters the room, watches everybody else. *Bruce Patterson*

Heard coming out of Mass at a little Irish church:
'Now that the Mass is in English instead of Latin, I
don't understand one word they are saying.' *Contributed by Anna M. Kirwan*

❋

'Where did I meet my Blonde? I opened my wallet
and there she was!' *Contributed by L. Winthrop*

❋

When I was eight years old my father told me
about the birds and the bees. The next day a bee
stung me and for seven months I thought I was
pregnant. *B. George*

❋

Age doesn't matter unless you're a cheese. *Billie Burke*

❋

Santa Claus has the right idea – visit people once a
year! *Victor Borge*

❋

Money isn't everything – but it will buy everything
it isn't. *Contributed by Cliff Hoskins*

❋

My husband calls me Claustrophobia because I live
in a constant fear of confinement. *Mother of 6 children/contributed by Leslie Page*

A boy in hospital told his mother when she went to visit him: 'It was God who operated on me. When I was in the big room there were two lady angels all dressed in white. Then two men angels came in. One of the men looked down my throat and said, "God, look at that child's tonsils!" And God looked and said. "I'll take them out at once!"' *Communication*

❀

Give and take but not for granted. *Contributed by Michael Tippett*

❀

Notice from the Boss to the firm's secretaries: 'There is a lot of bad spelling going on. If a word does not look right to you, kindly refer to your dictionary.' *Contributed by F. C. Pyke*

❀

He is a real pessimist – he could look at a dough-nut and only see the hole in it. *Contributed by W. G. Comer*

❀

Marriage is like a cafeteria – you take what looks good to you, and pay for it later. *Contributed by Andrew Cross*

❀

The real problem of your leisure is how to keep other people from using it. *Contributed by G. Adams*

What terrifies me is a future ruled by computers devising questions which can only be answered by computers. *Peter Ustinov/contributed by J. W. Richards*

❋

I believe the members of the dental profession are the only men who can tell a woman to open or close her mouth and get away with it. *Contributed by Victor Grant*

❋

A straight line is the shortest distance between two pints. *Contributed by F. J. Ball*

❋

If Harold Wilson had been captain of the Titanic, he'd have announced to the passengers after the ship hit the iceberg that they were simply stopping to take on ice. *Bob Young/contributed by Gordon Irving*

❋

They say that TV is still in its infancy, which probably explains why you have to get up so often to change it. *Contributed by Michael Hynes*

❋

Holidays: a time when there is not much on TV or radio − or the girls on the beach. *Contributed by Leslie Page*

Hell hath no fury like an habitual liar disbelieved when telling the truth. *Contributed by P. G. Tiptree*

✳

It isn't necessary to take a person's advice to make him feel good – all you have to do is ask it. *Contributed by Frances August*

✳

The worst unemployment area is often between the ears. *Communication*

✳

The older I get the less I pine for
Things that I have to stand in line for.
Richard Armour/contributed by L. I. Smith

✳

An umbrella – a shelter for one and a showerbath for two. *W. Hitchcock/contributed by V. A. Sharp*

✳

Wrinkles should merely indicate where smiles have been. *Lawrence Terne*

✳

The trouble with political jokes is that they are often elected to office. *Peter Elliot*

[61]

When the worm turns, it's generally because he's had instructions from the back seat. *Contributed by R. G. Hunt*

※

When I am good I am very very good, but when I am bad I am better. *Mae West/contributed by P. H. Buckley*

※

'It's not the work I enjoy,' said the taxi driver, 'it's the people I run into.' *Derek Holmes*

※

If ignorance is bliss, why aren't there more happy people? *S. White*

※

I drink on two occasions only – with fish and without fish. *Contributed by D. J. McCormack*

※

Boy handing report card to parent: 'Look this over and see if I can sue for defamation of character.' *John Marshall*

※

It is impossible to explain decency without being indecent. *George Bernard Shaw/contributed by J. R. Carr-Gregg*

A house-warming is a last hint to people who forgot to send wedding presents. *Jack Vine*

❋

A pleasure is none the less a pleasure because it does not please for ever. *Somerset Maugham/contributed by Keith Jones*

❋

A friend was travelling in someone else's car when he detected a noise in the engine.
'There's something wrong with your car,' he said. 'I can hear a funny noise in the engine.'
'Really?' asked the driver. 'In that case I'll switch the radio a bit louder and then you won't.' *Contributed by James Hilton*

❋

There's nothing keeps a woman on the straight and narrow so much as being made that way. *Contributed by E. Shaw*

❋

'I don't know if I like bathing beauties – I've never bathed any.' *Tommy Cooper/contributed by R. Prescott*

❋

A chap arrives at his office every morning and finds a molehill on his desk. All he has to do is make a mountain out of it by 5 PM. *Fred Allen/contributed by W. G. Comer*

Where there's a will there's always relations. *Contributed by Leonard Radcliffe*

❋

A youngster next door is not completely useless. At least five mothers use him as a bad example. *E. Dirkman*

❋

To want to meet an author because one likes his books is as ridiculous as wanting to meet the goose because one likes pâté de foie gras. *Attributed to Arthur Koestler/contributed by David Alexander*

❋

'Mean' — someone who switches his windscreen wipers off whenever he goes under a bridge. *Contributed by Tony Gadd*

❋

In its long quest for world peace, Russia has always stuck to its guns. *Saturday Evening Post/contributed by Symie Miller*

❋

A silly, childish game is one at which your wife can beat you. *Contributed by G. N. Dayman*

❋

Heredity — something you believe in if you have a bright child. *Contributed by M. Turpin*

Marriage has teeth – and teeth have toothache. *Jamaican proverb/contributed by Thelma Sangster*

❋

Just because we get girls here from the corset factory doesn't mean they are all genuine supporters. *Football club manager/contributed by Leslie Page*

❋

To one who said that he would rather vote for the Devil than John Wilkes, Wilkes replied, 'And if your friend is not standing?' *Contributed by Ian Jefferys*

❋

The new jet age can be defined as breakfast in London, lunch in New York, dinner in San Francisco and luggage in Bulawayo. *Derek Marshall*

❋

A girl can't get any more out of a sweater than she puts into it. *Bob Hope/contributed by Chris Wren*

❋

I've finally found out why my back has been giving me such trouble. Two weeks ago we got some of that ultra-modern office furniture and I've just learned I've been sitting in my wastebasket! *John E. Hogan*

Pedestrian — man whose wife beats him to the garage. *Contributed by A. Ward*

❋

A church is a hospital for sinners, not a museum for saints. *Abigail van Buren/contributed by O. Zahran*

❋

The shortest distance between two points is always under construction. *J. Adams*

❋

I don't understand women. They pay £4 for a slip and then worry if it shows! *Liddiard/contributed by L. Winthrop*

❋

In a London train compartment, a gentleman took out a cigar from his pocket. 'Excuse me, madam,' he said, to a little old lady opposite, 'May I smoke a cigar?'
'Do exactly as you would at home,' she replied.
'All right,' sighed the gentleman, and sadly put the cigar back into his breast pocket. *L. Bean*

❋

I expect that woman will be the last thing civilized by man. *George Meredith*

❋

Discretion is raising one's eyebrows instead of the roof. *Contributed by G. N. Dayman*

Every really busy man should take a year's holiday at 40 to recover physique and poise of mind. *George Bernard Shaw*

❋

Good breeding consists of concealing how much we think of ourselves and how little we think of the other person. *Mark Twain*

❋

A big shot is a fellow who has his name printed on company letterheads because no one can read his signature. *Patricia Moody*

❋

The brain is a wonderful thing. It never stops functioning from the time you are born until the moment you stand up to make a speech. *Dr L. Binder*

❋

Overheard in the women's bar at the golf club: 'Girls, I have a marvellous recipe for goulash. When I mention it to my husband, he says, "Oh gosh. Let's eat out." ' *Contributed by Bill Boorne*

❋

A mini-skirt gives men an untaxable fringe benefit. *Contributed by Peter Lindsay*

A stitch in time is usually a surprise to a married man. *Contributed by Andrew Cross*

❈

The only time a husband and wife see eye to eye is when they are the same height. *N. Castle*

❈

A man who is old enough to know better is always on the look out for a girl who doesn't. *Contributed by P. H. Buckley*

❈

The trouble with bucket seats is that not everyone has the same size bucket. *O. Mason*

❈

It is much easier to be critical than correct. *Disraeli/contributed by G. J. McGreeny*

❈

A pedestrian is a person who can't remember where he parked his car. *Contributed by R. G. Hunt*

❈

Car insurance rates are higher for single young men. If they're so reckless, why don't they get married? *A. Edbrook*

❈

He calls his wife Peninsula – a long neck looking out to see. *Contributed by S. J. Hallett*

1969

✳

A woman chatted to friends at a bridge party: 'My resolution this year is never to repeat gossip, so for heaven's sake, listen the FIRST time.' *R. Love*

✳

I find it hard keeping a secretary. Either they get married or they remind me that I am ... *Contributed by Leslie Page*

✳

Glamour girl to male fellow worker: 'Yes, I can tell you how I got my rise, but I don't think it will help you much!' *M. H. Beuchat*

✳

Sign in a laundry window. 'Don't kill your wife — let us do your dirty work.' *S. Towers*

✳

My son has heard me bang on the bathroom door to my wife and say 'God, are you still in there?' so often, that now he believes God lives in our bathroom. *Contributed by C. J. McManus*

We hope that when the insects take over the world they will remember with gratitude how we took them along on all our picnics. *Bill Vaughan*

Every time we listen to the top fifty records we shudder to think what the bottom fifty must sound like. *C. Street*

❋

'I never try to make Henry do anything he doesn't want to do . . . I just try to make the alternative as unpleasant as possible!' *A. Baker*

❋

Penitent to priest: 'How far is it right to go with a girl?' Priest to penitent: 'As far as you like, my son – provided you keep walking.' *Contributed by John Biggs-Davison, MP*

❋

An MP said we should pay our taxes with a smile. Wish I'd known that last April – I sent cash. *S. Norwood*

❋

The war between the sexes can never be brought to a successful conclusion because there's too much fraternizing with the enemy. *Contributed by P. H. Buckley*

❋

It's funny that a wife who can see right through you doesn't notice a missing button. *Chris Hipple*

A wife, complaining her husband hadn't taken a good look at her in five years, remarked: 'If anything happened to me, I don't think he'd be able to identify the body.' *N. Wells*

❋

The other planets may not be able to support life, but it isn't all that easy on this one either. *Contributed by R. G. Hunt*

❋

Mrs Karl Marx is said to have observed, at the end of a long and rather bleak life, how much better it would have been if dear Karl had made some capital instead of writing so much about it. *Harold Macmillan/contributed by John Rhodes*

❋

Boss to employee: 'In a way I'll be sorry to lose you. You've been just like a son to me; insolent, surly and unappreciative.' *P. Thomas*

❋

Our customary salutation 'Good Day' is a vestige of an agricultural society where people were asking for good weather. I expect city dwellers eventually to greet one another with the phrase 'Low Prices'. *Walter Hamilton/contributed by David Alexander*

❋

A committee is a 'cul-de-sac' to which ideas are lured and quietly strangled. *John A. Lincoln*

Never proclaim your future to those who know your past. *Contributed by George Clouston*

❇

It's amazing how a woman who can spot a smudge of lipstick on a man's collar at 15 paces can't see a pair of garage doors 20 feet wide. *E. Dirkman*

❇

A lot of fellows who drive as if they owned the road don't even own the car. *Irish Digest*

❇

When I was 40, my doctor advised me that a man in his forties shouldn't play tennis. I heeded his advice carefully and could hardly wait until I reached 50 to start again. *J. H. Black*

❇

I took a course in speed reading, learning to read straight down the middle of the page, and was able to read 'War and Peace' in 20 minutes. It's about Russia. *Woody Allen/contributed by Dewi Lewis*

❇

A perfectionist takes infinite pains and often gives them to other people. *Contributed by G. N. Dayman*

❇

Some are born poor, but parents of students get poor by degrees. *Contributed by F. Hirst*

The scientists split the atom – and now the atom is splitting us. *Quentin Reynolds*

※

Psychiatrists say girls tend to marry men like their fathers. That is probably the reason mothers cry at weddings. *Contributed by Leslie Page*

※

We prefer the old-fashioned alarm clock to the kind that awakens you with soft music or a gentle whisper. If there's one thing we can't stand in the morning it's hypocrisy. *Bill Vaughan*

※

A man being introduced to Churchill said: 'I am so thrilled to meet you in the flesh,' to which Churchill replied, 'I am never without it!' *Contributed by Arthur J. Lewis, MP*

※

Henry VIII was a fresh heir fiend. *Contributed by Andrew Page*

※

Before making up your mind to retire, it is highly advisable to stay home for a week and watch daytime television shows. *Frieda Henry*

※

A man is known by the company he thinks nobody knows he keeps. *Contributed by Andrew Cross*

Girl to date: 'Gosh! It's just like Romeo and Juliet – my father hates you!' *A. R. Cross*

❋

Husband to wife as they start out to dinner, leaving their son with a babysitter: 'I still say, when they begin to ask for a blonde instead of a brunette, they're old enough to stay alone!' *Robert E. Wilson*

❋

From a house magazine report on the firm's annual sports day: Mrs Smith won the women's hammer-throwing event by hurling the hammer 75 feet. Mr Smith won the 100 yards sprint. *S. Conway*

❋

When you get to the end of your tether – tie a knot in it and hang on! *Contributed by L. Winthrop*

❋

It is not what they think of me that matters, but what I think of them. *Queen Victoria/contributed by C. Neville*

❋

No man can understand why a woman should prefer a good reputation to a good time. *Contributed by Pat Buckley*

During a domestic row, a husband said: 'Now lets talk this matter over reasonably!'
Wife: 'No! That way you always win.' *Contributed by D. M. Clark*

✳

It might well be true that men are more intelligent than women, but you never see a woman marrying a dumb man because of his shape. *Contributed by Leslie Page*

✳

Sign on a dust-cart: satisfaction guaranteed or twice your rubbish back. *F. Taylor*

The worst moment for an atheist is when he feels grateful and has no one to thank. *Wendy Ward*

❊

An air traveller weighed himself on the automatic weighing machine standing next to the 'accident insurance' slot machine he had just used and received a weight card on the back of which was printed 'a recent investment will pay high dividends'. *Contributed by F. C. Pyke*

❊

Stating the case for a second crematorium for Leicester, a city alderman told this week's meeting of the town council that the present unit would not be able to cope with the weight of work much longer. He added: 'If anything went wrong we would be in grave difficulties.' *Contributed by Mrs K. Waterfield*

❊

Chivalry is the attitude of a man towards somebody else's wife. *Contributed by Gordon Irving*

❊

I have three reasons for not drinking overmuch. First, the sin of it, second the shame, and third the sickness. *John Philpot Curran/Toptable Talk*

❊

Egotism and mumps are very much alike, except that the swelling shows in different places. *Contributed by Ronald Allison*

Discussing the break-up of a celebrated *ménage à deux*, a friend of the unhappy woman explained: 'Helen thought she was being kept when she was merely being detained.' *Contributed by A. S. Subramaniam*

❋

A synonym is a word you use when you can't spell the first word you thought of. *B. Bacharach*

❋

Notice in a London furrier's: 'A small deposit secures any fur until your husband gives in.' *Contributed by Dewi Lewis*

❋

Old age is like everything else. To make a success of it you've got to start young. *Contributed by W. Lawrence*

❋

One man in a thousand is a leader of men, the rest are followers of women. *Harry Stanley/contributed by John Rhodes*

❋

An ounce of judicious praise is worth a ton of indiscriminate censure. *Duke of Wellington/ contributed by E. Paton-Smith*

Behind the success of this man is the guiding hand of a remarkable woman, and there'll be hell to pay if his wife finds out. *Jack Bentley/contributed by Gordon Irving*

❅

Many are called but few get up. *Contributed by Robin Andrews*

❅

On the day when the lotus bloomed, alas, my mind was straying and I knew it not. *Rabindranath Tagore*

❅

He went to the top because he was careful to conceal those qualifications which otherwise would have kept him at the bottom. *Contributed by C. S. Neale*

❅

Overheard after the wedding. 'They should be very happy. They're both so in love with him.' *I. D. Gest*

❅

Adam and Eve – originators of the loose-leaf system. *Contributed by Andrew Page*

❅

The trouble with antiques is their modern prices. *C. Bell*

Men are usually more careful about the breed of their horses and dogs than of their children. *W. Penn*

※

A successful man is one who makes more money than his wife can spend. A successful woman is one who can find such a man. *Contributed by M. M. Owen*

※

He was so worried when he read somewhere that smoking could cause cancer he gave up reading. *Contributed by Anna M. Kirwan*

※

The best committee consists of two members, one of whom is ill. *Contributed by G. Wynne Thomas*

※

Sociology: the study of people who do not need to be studied by people who do. *E. S. Turner/contributed by D. Alexander*

※

One employee to another: 'My mistake was buying shares in the company. Now I worry about the awful work I'm turning out.' *Contributed by Dewi Lewis*

It is difficult to make a woman believe that even a bargain costs money. *Contributed by Desmond Clark*

✻

Two young women were talking about their mothers-in-law. One was quite effusive in praise of hers. 'She's an angel,' she said. The other was silent for a moment. Then she said, 'You're lucky, mine is still with us.' *S. Yuill/contributed by P. Anderson*

✻

Overheard at Sandown: 'I haven't seen Johnny for ages. Has he married again?' 'No, but I hear he's got a loose box at Melton.' *Contributed by A. W. Urquhart*

✻

Intoxication: When you feel sophisticated and cannot pronounce it. *D. Farmer*

✻

The trouble with the family of today is that everybody wears the trousers. *Don Fraser/contributed by B. French*

✻

Sign in a barber's window: We need your head to carry on our business. *Contributed by B. J. Fielding*

There are few women auctioneers because it is difficult for a woman to say loudly, 'Will anyone make me an offer?' *Contributed by Leslie Page*

✳

She didn't know her husband drank until she saw him sober. *Robert Jansen*

✳

One time a man who saved money was a miser. Now he's a genius. *Contributed by W. G. Comer*

✳

How long a minute is depends on which side of the bathroom door you happen to be. *R. Porter*

✳

How is it that people you can easily see through never sit in front of you at the cinema. *Contributed by L. I. Smith*

✳

Definition of progress: Movement in a direction of which you approve. *Contributed by Colonel R. B. Oram*

✳

An optimist is a man who does a crossword puzzle in ink. *Contributed by W. Lawrence*

Wanted: Job as secretary. No bad habits ... willing to learn. *Contributed by Andrew Cross*

※

A British judge was visiting Tanzania, where the people often carry bundles on their heads. In Dar-es-Salaam he saw an official in formal dress wearing his top hat upside down. The judge whispered that this wasn't the way to wear a top hat. 'But my dear judge,' the man replied, 'I am not wearing the hat, I'm carrying it.' *Leonard Lyons/ contributed by A. S. Subramaniam*

※

You don't have to dress up to shoot – for instance, you get grouse in braces. *Contributed by L. Winthrop*

※

The trouble with opportunity is that it always looks bigger going than coming. *Bremer/contributed by J. Bradbury*

※

Sign outside a dance hall at High Wycombe: 'Good clean entertainment every night except Monday.' *Contributed by J. G. Lentell*

※

A bore being introduced to President de Gaulle said: 'We last met in Algiers in '43, *mon Général*,' to which came the reply: 'How kind of you to remember.' *Contributed by John Biggs-Davison, MP*

Some girls don't care for a man's company unless he owns it. *John Barrow*

❋

A young child, tired of hearing the admiration expressed for her charming elder sister, exclaimed loudly: 'Well, all the dogs always go for me.' *Contributed by M. Buchholtz*

❋

Waitress: A woman who thinks money grows on trays. *G. White*

❋

A camel is a horse designed by a committee. *Contributed by Dewi Lewis*

❋

Life is an everlasting struggle to keep money coming in and hair and teeth from coming out. *Contributed by Andrew Cross*

❋

Overheard: 'I got a new car for the wife. Quite a good swop.' *Yorkshire Evening Post/contributed by F. Hirst*

❋

Experience is the name everyone gives to their mistakes. *Oscar Wilde*

The essence of any blue material is timing. If you sit on it, it becomes vulgar. *Danny La Rue/contributed by Gordon Irving*

❋

I'm so underpaid, I'm the only man I know who can cash his cheque on the bus. *Alan Sandquist*

❋

Woman driver to companion, after parking car: 'That's close enough . . . we can walk to the kerb,' *Contributed by J. F. Wilson*

❋

As soon as a man acquires fairly good sense it is said he is an old fogey. *E. W. Howe/contributed by J. Forrest*

❋

Women's clothes nowadays are all strip and no tease. *Peter Ustinov/contributed by D. M. Clark*

❋

An old farmer, asked why he had never married, explained: 'Well, I'd rather go through life wanting something I didn't have than having something I didn't want.' *Contributed by A. S. Subramaniam*

❋

A fool and his money are frequently invited places. *Contributed by M. M. Owen*

A low cut dress should be like a garden gate – to guard the property without blocking the view.
Contributed by Pat Buckley

❋

Kissing don't last: cookery do. *Contributed by Caradoc Evans*

❋

It isn't being a grandfather that makes you feel old – it's being married to a grandmother. *Contributed by D. Griffiths*

❋

Salesman: 'Madam, I'd like to show you a little item your neighbours said you couldn't afford.' *V. L. Guffey*

❋

The head waiter came to the table to inquire if the *Fondue Bourguignonne* was all right.
'Of course it's all right,' replied the hostess of the party, 'we're cooking it ourselves aren't we?' *Contributed by J. Dible*

❋

Do infants have as much fun in infancy as adults do in adultery? *Murray Banks/contributed by John Rhodes*

The really well-adjusted man is one who can enjoy the scenery when he has to take a detour. *G. Collins*

❋

This country may be on the road to ruin but it will never get there with the present traffic congestion. *Contributed by R. G. Hunt*

❋

If my husband ever puts me on a pedestal, it will be so that I can reach the ceiling to paint it! *Contributed by L. Winthrop*

❋

We recently attended a wedding where the bride was six months pregnant – the guests all threw puffed rice. *R. J. Fredrikson*

❋

The fellow who thinks he knows it all is especially annoying to those of us who do. *Peter Holmes*

❋

The time you enjoyed wasting was not wasted time. *Contributed by J. S. O'Halloran*

❋

The sad thing about ulcers is that you can have them and still not be a success. *William Henry*

A sheriff in America confiscated a group of slot machines on the basis of a law banning the use of steel traps for catching dumb animals. *Ian White*

A mother takes twenty years to make a man of her boy and another woman makes a fool of him in twenty minutes. *Contributed by J. F. Wilson*

The modern husband believes that a woman's place is in the home – and expects her to go there immediately after work. *Richard Cooper*

Universities are full of knowledge; the freshmen bring in a little and the seniors take none away, and knowledge accumulates. *A. L. Lowell/ contributed by Arthur J. Lewis, MP*

The trouble with tranquillizers is that you find yourself being nice to people you don't like. *M. Bushman*

Most people buy a new car because they have to pay cash on the bus. *Contributed by Leslie Page*

There is talk of eliminating violence on TV. Well! There goes the 11 o'clock news. *John Marshall*

A woman told the marriage counsellor that her husband's complaint that he led a dog's life was probably well-founded. 'He comes into the house with muddy feet, tracks across my clean floors, barks at nothing, growls at his food, and makes himself comfortable on my best furniture.' *Contributed by M. Subramaniam*

※

Money may not buy happiness, but with it you can be miserable in comfort. *Contributed by Andrew Cross*

※

If you've half a mind to watch TV, that is enough. *W. H. Lewis*

※

Some women worship their husbands – they place burnt offerings before them three times a day. *William Holder*

※

An executive is a big gun who has succeeded in not being fired. *Contributed by Dewi Lewis*

※

To be born a gentleman is an accident but to die a gentleman is an achievement. *Contributed by G. H. Seymour*

'I don't want to scare you,' the seven-year-old informed his teacher, 'but my daddy says if I don't get better marks somebody is going to get spanked.' *Kathleen Murray*

✻

A beauty parlour is a place where business is always improving. *Contributed by W. G. Comer*

✻

'Shall I get rid of this old file now that the matter is finally disposed of, sir?'
'Certainly, but make a copy of everything before you destroy it.' *Contributed by Anna M. Kirwan*

✻

Sign on a bookstore going out of business: 'Words failed us.' *Gordon Gregory*

✻

The irrelevance of women is their greatest charm: no doubt while Nero fiddled, his wife fussed over burnt toast. *Contributed by R. J. Austin*

✻

An optimist is a husband who goes to the registrar every year to see if his marriage licence has expired. *Henry Leabo*

Fools rush in where angels fear to tread; and all the angels are in heaven but few of the fools are dead. *James Thurber/contributed by Loraine Hoskins*

❋

The hardest task of a girl's life is to prove to a man that his intentions are serious. *Helen Rowland/contributed by Desmond Clark*

❋

Imagination is what makes you think you're having a wonderful time when you're only spending money. *Daniel Rider*

❋

Intuition is that which enables a woman to arrive at the most infallible irrevocable decision, without the aid of reason, judgement or discussion. *Contributed by Tony Gadd*

❋

The Texas oil man's daughter returned from college and he was showing her around their new mansion. They stopped at the swimming pool to watch several athletic young men cavorting on the diving board. 'Oh, daddy,' she exclaimed, 'you've stocked it for me!' *Bill Johnstone*

❋

Taxes: Status woe. *John Clark*

Psychologists who advise parents to spend more time with their children are just trying to drum up future business. *John Vaughan*

✳

If a lot of people said what they think, they'd be speechless. *Wall Street Journal*

✳

Youth would be an ideal state if it came a little later in life. *Lord Asquith/contributed by D. M. Goldman*

✳

An atheist is a man who has no invisible means of support. *John Buchan/contributed by Gordon Irving*

✳

The rich man and his daughter are soon parted. *Kim Hubbard/contributed by John G. Hay*

✳

The sweetest music to a woman's ears is made by another woman playing second fiddle. *J. W. Cuthbert*

✳

A woman who thinks that she is intelligent demands equal rights with men. A woman who is intelligent does not. *Contributed by Andrew Cross*

We have three children. My wife refuses to have a fourth as she has heard that every fourth child born into the world is Chinese. *Contributed by L. Winthrop*

❋

Psychology tells us that it is bad to be an orphan, terrible to be an only child, damaging to be the youngest, crushing to be in the middle, taxing to be the oldest. There is no way out except to be born an adult. *George Long*

❋

A crematorium circularized the undertakers and church officials in its neighbourhood asking them 'in the interests of efficiency to ensure that funeral cortèges arrived dead on time, particularly during the month of August when only a skeleton staff is on duty.' *Contributed by John E. H. Coates*

❋

A third of what we eat keeps us alive; the other two-thirds keeps the doctor alive. *Contributed by W. A. Clarke*

❋

Practical nurse: one who marries a wealthy patient and then retires. *Dorothy Rider*

❋

The nearest thing to an honest politician is one who, when he's bought, stays bought. *Kathleen Lindner*

Woman would be more charming if one could fall into her arms without falling into her hands. *James H. Hanson*

✻

A diplomat is one who can tell you to go to hell so tactfully that you start packing for the trip. *Michael Robbins*

✻

Father to Mother: 'At least this report card proves he isn't taking any mind-expanding drugs.' *Beverly Winchall*

✻

Husband overheard as he answered the phone: 'She's not at home, Mrs Barlow. Would you like to leave a rumour?' *L. Henry*

✻

Nothing shows the British spirit of compromise better than the motorist straddling two lanes of traffic. *Len Deighton/contributed by E. Shaw*

✻

The secret of patience is doing something else in the meantime. *Bill Henry*

✻

Man to his wife: 'It isn't true that I don't like your family. As a matter of fact I prefer your mother-in-law to my own.' *Contributed by Anna M. Kirwan*

Most men have two great ambitions: first to own their own home and second to own a car so that they can get away from home. *Contributed by W. G. Comer*

❋

Traffic's so slow in London that if you want to hit a pedestrian you have to get out of your car. *Arnold Glasgow*

❋

It is all right for a person to talk to himself if he doesn't take what he says too seriously. *M. Fox*

❋

'Remember the good old days,' sighed the medical student, 'when having a change of heart didn't mean an operation?' *Contributed by R. Prescott*

❋

Man at door to market researcher: 'That's my opinion, and I can give you my wife's even though she's not here. It would be just the opposite of mine.' *Patricia Moody*

❋

Woman to friend: 'I never vote. It's such a relief not to feel responsible for anything that happens in Parliament.' *Contributed by Andrew Cross*

The trouble with the world today is that 'The Pilgrim's Progress' is superseded by the Pill's grim progress! *Contributed by J. H. Thomas*

＊

Marriage is a committee of two with the power to add to their number. *Contributed by P. B. D. Bunyan*

＊

Nonchalance is the ability to act like an owl after having behaved like an ass. *Contributed by P. Smith*

＊

Notice in a local newspaper: 'There is still time for last minute entries for the Festival Queen — don't be shy, you won't be asked to wear a swimming costume.' *Contributed by B. B. Smith*

＊

Before letting your mind wander make sure it isn't too weak to be out alone. *Contributed by Michael Gynes*

＊

One of the merits of the Austin Maxi: it has seats which fold down to make one large bed, which should appeal to the young man about to start a family. *Report in British Industry Week/contributed by J. G. Lentell*

Most women prefer to marry a man with a strong will – made out to them. *Contributed by R. G. Hunt*

I never forget a face, but in your case I'm willing to make an exception. *Groucho Marx*

A policeman at the House of Commons was asked if the chaplain ever prayed for the members.
'No, sir,' he replied. 'He just looks at them and then prays for the country.' *Contributed by C. Subramaniam*

The woman who is absent from the bridge game gets the most slams. *I. Chase*

✳

Travelling by plane from London to Glasgow I was engrossed in a book on bridge when the the stewardess stopped and looked over my shoulder. 'That must be a fascinating love story you're reading,' she said. Startled, I looked at the chapter heading with fresh eyes – 'Free Responses after an Original Pass.' *T. R. Soames*

✳

A woman was driven all over Europe by her husband every holiday for 40 years. During a visit to Cyprus they did their sight-seeing by chauffeur-driven car. 'I don't like a hired car,' she complained, 'you have to be polite to the driver.' *Contributed by Colonel R. B. Oram*

✳

He who laughs last is usually the last to get the joke. *Terry Cohen*

✳

A London coroner's verdict in the case of an Aberdonian who was run over by a bus in Piccadilly Circus when he stepped forward to pick up a three-penny piece – Death through natural causes. *Contributed by E. F. Balloch*

✳

Fun is like life insurance: the older you get the more it costs. *Kim Hubbard/contributed by Dewi Lewis*

Unrequited love is like appendicitis – it hurts like mad until you get it out of your system. *Contributed by M. Marks*

✳

Young lady acknowledging an introduction, 'Oh, I've heard so much about you, now I'd like to hear your side.' *W. Phillips*

✳

'Now,' said the golf professional, 'suppose you just go through the motions without hitting the ball.'
'But that's precisely the difficulty I'm trying to overcome,' said his pupil. *E. Sutcliffe*

✳

Psychiatry must be the only business where the customer is always wrong. *Contributed by Michael Hynes*

✳

Wife to husband: 'Of course I want you to have opinions of your own. I just don't want to hear them.' *J. Carroll*

✳

Well timed silence has more eloquence than speech. *Contributed by Ronald Allison*

✳

A letter signed by an Undertaker – Yours eventually. *Contributed by D. J. McCormack*

One trouble with the government is that it seems to think the individual owes it a living. *Joan Baez*

❋

You can do very little with faith, but you can do nothing without it. *Contributed by John Sutro*

❋

They are incompatible. The less income he has, the less pattable she becomes. *Contributed by D. Clark*

❋

The only man who seriously tried to raise politicians to a higher level was Guy Fawkes. *Contributed by G. W. Adams*

❋

Television is called a medium because so little of it is rare or well done. *Contributed by R. G. Hunt*

❋

If a man never changes his opinions he never corrects his mistakes. *Contributed by E. South*

❋

Parents who never strike their children in anger probably can't run fast enough. *R. J. Miller*

Diplomacy is the art of letting someone have your way. *Contributed by Ian P. Spratling*

❋

Divorce simply proves whose mother was right in the first place. *Contributed by W. A. Clarke*

❋

At a dinner-party, a shy young man had been trying to think of something nice to say to his hostess. At last he saw his chance when she turned to him and remarked. 'What a small appetite you have, Mr Whyte.' 'To sit next to you,' he replied gallantly, 'would cause any man to lose his appetite.' *S. Pine*

❋

When success turns a person's head he is facing failure. *Contributed by D. M. Goldman*

❋

Last year I was conceited but now I'm cured; this year I'm perfect. *Contributed by J. Dible*

❋

Sign on a supermarket manager's door — Trust in God, all others cash. *Contributed by F. Hirst*

❋

The honeymoon is over when the bridegroom stops helping with the dishes and does them himself. *Robert Wagner/contributed by John G. Hay*

A woman will give sixpence to a beggar in order to spend five pounds on a new hat with a clear conscience. *Contributed by Richard Austin*

❋

Boy friend: 'Your sister and I are going to be married.'
Younger brother: 'Have you only just found that out?' *Contributed by Arthur J. Lewis, MP*

❋

A mother spends the first fifteen years teaching her son to be a man; the son spends the next fifteen years teaching his mother that he is. *L. Robinson*

❋

Remove from a woman her grievances and she loses her zest for life. *Contributed by C. W. Langford*

❋

Seen on a Jumble Sale notice: A chance to be rid of anything you don't want, yet too good to throw away. Bring your husband. *Contributed by J. G. Lentell*

❋

A Headmaster tells of an examination in which the class were asked to define a 'virgin'. One boy wrote – a nun in confinement. *Contributed by Pat Buckley*

A lot of people get credit for being well-behaved because they don't have the money to do otherwise. *Contributed by Andrew Cross*

❋

A boy's love comes from a full heart; a man's is more often the result of a full stomach. *Contributed by C. J. Fleetwood*

❋

Wife to husband: 'I took one of those compatibility tests in the magazine today, and you failed.' *Contributed by Dewi Lewis*

❋

A chance remark is anything a man manages to say when two women are talking. *Contributed by R. G. Hunt*

❋

Undoubtedly the best time for the Government to have undertaken the decimalization of our currency would have been when all the old people were dead. *Contributed by Barnett Field*

❋

A fellow who's always declaring he's no fool usually has his surprises. *Contributed by M. H. Love*

A boy's voice changes when he becomes a man; a girl's voice changes when she becomes a wife. *Wilfred E. Beaver/contributed by W. A. Clarke*

✳

Automation will never beat the wastepaper basket in speeding up office work. *R. Allen/contributed by J. H. Thomas*

✳

The most recent Pill weighs over 250lb – you roll it against the bedroom door and no one can get in. *Lonnie Donegan/contributed by Dr B. Weir*

✳

It was said of Alfred de Musset that he steadily became more and more absinthe-minded. *Contributed by P. Anderson*

✳

There is far too much emphasis on sex these days – it should be put in its proper perspective like food and drink – breakfast time, lunch time, tea time and supper time. *Contributed by P. I. Robinson*

✳

Nothing ruins an old boys' reunion like the fellow who has managed to stay young looking and get rich at the same time. *M. Loughlin*

People go on holiday to forget things, and when they open their cases they find out they have. *Contributed by John C. Hay*

✿

My wife cooks for fun. For food we go out to a restaurant. *Tommy Cooper/contributed by Gordon Irving*

✿

I find it very hard to support the government and a wife on one income. *Contributed by W. G. Comer*

✿

A cold can be like a committee – sometimes the eyes have it and sometimes the nose. *Contributed by B. Ward*

✿

It isn't tying himself to one woman that a man dreads when he thinks of marrying, it's separating himself from all the others. *Helen Rowland/contributed by Desmond Clark*

✿

Father to daughter: 'I think he's getting serious. He asked me how much you earned!' *K. Reynolds/contributed by L. Winthrop*

✿

People may say what they like about the decay of Christianity: the religious system that produced green Chartreuse can never really die. *Saki/contributed by P. Alexander*

In eating, a third of the stomach should be filled with food, a third with drink and the rest left empty. *Contributed by C. Moss*

1970

❋

I have suffered many things in this life, most of which have never happened. *G. W. Gates*

❋

In Ireland they call you a Queer if you forsake drinking for women. *Phil the Fluter/contributed by L. Winthrop*

In the age of the moonshot we carry on institutions of Gladstone and Disraeli. *Mrs Grimmond/contributed by E. F. Ballock*

❋

Most men never bring the boss home to dinner because she is there already. *Contributed by R. G. Hunt*

❋

Feminine touch: an outstretched hand every Friday evening. *Contributed by Dewi Lewis*

❋

Holidays are great levellers. The person who takes one returns home just as broke as the person who stayed at home because he couldn't afford to go. *Contributed by V. A. Sharp*

❋

I like Wagner's music better than anybody's. It is so loud that one can talk the whole time without other people hearing what one says. *Oscar Wilde/contributed by John Rhodes*

❋

There is a difference between beauty and charm. A beautiful woman is one I notice. A charming woman is one who notices me. *John Erskine*

If you put a clock on the Leaning Tower of Pisa you would have the time *and* the inclination. *Contributed by B. Ward*

※

Notice on a farm gate in Breconshire: 'Beware of the bull. Survivors will be prosecuted.' *Contributed by H. J. Hewson*

※

Nobody is happy all the time but that is no excuse for being miserable. *Contributed by L. Harris*

※

As soon as you cannot keep anything from a woman you love her. *Paul Geraldy*

※

Three prime ministers with a difference – Benjamin Disraeli delighted in planting trees; William Ewart Gladstone had a passion for felling trees; Harold Wilson's inclination for forestry is confined to 'bond-fires'. *Contributed by A. W. Urquhart*

※

From an advertisement for psychologists: 'Professional men and women today can choose the specific area of activity in which they wish to work in government service, where the scope for psychologists is probably greater than in any other single organization in the country.' *Contributed by D. K. O. Ullmann*

Give some people an inch and they think they are rulers. *Contributed by W. A. Clarke*

✳

If you are in a pub in Northern Ireland, don't make the mistake of asking for a Gin and Bitter Orange. *Contributed by Anna M. Kirwan*

✳

Every man who is high up loves to think that he has done it all himself; and the wife smiles and lets it go at that. *Sir James M. Barrie/contributed by Gordon Irving*

✳

My wife says that you can't take your money with you, but at the rate she spends it we'll be leaving early! *Contributed by Kevin Donovan*

✳

It is anti-social to pass your cigarettes around: everyone prefers his own brand of suicide. *Shirley Conlan/contributed by Anna M. Kirwan*

✳

Ghandi was once asked: 'What do you think of Western civilization?' I think it would be a good idea,' he replied. *Contributed by Desmond Clark*

There's no such thing as strangers, only friends we haven't met. *Contributed by J. S. O'Halloran*

✳

Mere marriage is not morality. *George Bernard Shaw/contributed by David Alexander*

✳

What Roman Catholics call contraceptives are used by Protestants on every conceivable occasion. *Contributed by Edmund Ellis*

✳

The great advantage of being in a rut is that when one is in a rut one knows exactly where one is. *Alan Bennett/contributed by David Alexander*

✳

She wore far too much rouge last night and not quite enough clothes. That is always a sign of despair in a woman. *From 'An Ideal Husband'/contributed by R. Laurie*

✳

According to a recent leaflet about the nervousness of some animals at sudden noises, farmers should '. . . avoid calling their cows in a loud voice, always low'. *Contributed by P. A. Sterlini*

✳

A person who buys a second-hand car soon discovers how hard it is to drive a bargain. *C. Hardy*

He has definite tastes about women's clothes. He can't stand his wife in anything over four-pounds-ten. *Contributed by Desmond Clark*

✻

When a woman says she can read you like a book you are finished. *Contributed by W. G. Comer*

✻

Marriage is a form of emotional insurance: divorce, a realization of one's surrender value. *Contributed by B. J. Hargreaves*

✻

A glutton: A man who sends out for a copy of 'Playboy' on his honeymoon. *600 Magazine/contributed by Gordon Irving*

✻

A man was suing his wife for divorce on the grounds that she was emotionally immature. 'Why, Judge,' he said, 'do you know that she is so immature that she burst into the bathroom one day while I was in the tub and sank all my boats.' *Contributed by Edward Atkinson*

✻

Happy is the man with a wife to tell him what to do and a secretary to do it. *Lord Mancroft/contributed by Dewi Lewis*

Success is making more money to pay the taxes you wouldn't have to pay if you didn't make so much money. *Contributed by R. G. Hunt*

Not to take women seriously is to ask for trouble. To take them seriously is to get it. *Contributed by L. Harris*

The rainy days for which a man saves usually come during his holiday. *Contributed by John G. Hay*

Common sense is instinct. Enough of it is genius. *Contributed by Philip Pine*

'Yes,' said the wife, 'my husband is a great help around the house. At the moment he's taking the baby's nap for him.' *Leo Aikman/contributed by Dewi Lewis*

A woman becomes more beautiful in front of the eyes she loves: she ceases to be in front of the eyes she doesn't. *Contributed by Omar Zahren*

Southern Irish barmaid to English tourist: 'Sorry, sir, the bar doesn't open for another half hour. Would you like a drink while you're waiting?' *Contributed by J. W. Beaumont*

You can usually tell if a girl has a gift for painting. It shows on her face. *Contributed by B. Ward*

Babies are angels whose wings grow shorter as their legs grow longer. *Contributed by W. G. Comer*

A psychiatrist received a card from a patient who was on holiday. It read – 'Having a wonderful time ... why?' *Contributed by Andrew Cross*

Owner of a new puppy: 'My dog is fully house-trained – he does everything in the house.' *Contributed by E. F. Balloch*

❀

'You know you told your mother to look on the house as her own? Well, she's decided to sell it.' *Contributed by Colin Fenn*

❀

Sign at an Irish auctioneers: The highest bidder to be the buyer, unless someone bids more. *Contributed by J. S. O'Halloran*

❀

After reading memorial stones in a cemetery, you wonder where they bury the sinners. *Contributed by W. A. Clarke*

❀

In Communist countries you do as you are told. In non-Communist countries you do as you like as long as you do as you are told. *Contributed by Eric N. Osborne*

❀

A pessimist is someone whose environment takes on the shape of his worries. *Contributed by Ricky Reeves*

One young man spent so much money on his girl that he finally had to marry her for his money. *Contributed by Desmond Clark*

❋

Politics are for those who have a great regard for themselves, little regard for others and no regard for the truth. *Contributed by L. Harris*

❋

The great majority of the English move inside much too narrow an ambit of drinks, and many lives move between beer and tea. *Douglas Woodruff*

❋

Women are like pianos – some of them are upright, the rest are grand. *Contributed by R. Herbert Smith*

❋

A smile is a curve which can set a lot of things straight. *Contributed by D. M. Goldman*

❋

A soft drink turneth away company. *Oliver Herford*

❋

The first thing the modern baby learns at its mother's knee is not to ladder her tights. *Contributed by R. Prescott*

People are like small pins – they are absolutely useless when they lose their heads. *Contributed by S. Miller*

✳

Psychiatrists are doctors who do not like the sight of blood. *Contributed by J. Webster*

✳

When a girl has pretty teeth she never fails to see the joke. *Contributed by Philip Pine*

✳

Wouldn't it be nice if two weeks holiday seemed to last as long as two weeks on a diet? *Earl Wilson/contributed by John G. Hay*

✳

A successful executive is one who can delegate all the responsibility, shift all the blame, and take all the credit. *Contributed by Gordon Irving*

✳

An aborigine received a present of a new boomerang, but he hasn't yet succeeded in throwing away the old one. *Contributed by B. Phillips*

✳

As far as money is concerned most of us have very little to complain about. *Contributed by Alan Webber*

Don't covet your neighbour's wife: you may get her. *Contributed by Mark Haymon*

❈

Seen on a church notice board: If you're tired of sin come in. Scrawled underneath – If not, ring Bayswater 1238. *Ted Ray/contributed by F. Albury*

❈

A highbrow is one who, when he sees a sausage, thinks of Picasso. *Contributed by B. J. Hargreaves*

❈

No dog can go as fast as the money you bet on him. *Bud Flanagan/contributed by Arthur J. Lewis, MP*

❈

My wife has been given so many pep pills by the doctor that I have to take some to keep up with her. *Contributed by Anna M. Kirwan*

❈

Women are wiser than men because they know less and understand more. *Contributed by A. P. Robinson*

❈

A husband is a lover with the nerve extracted. *Helen Rowland/contributed by Ronald K. Gough*

Moral indignation is often jealousy with a halo. *Contributed by W. A. Clarke*

✻

It isn't the cold girl who gets the fur coat. *John Taylor*

✻

From an advertisement: On our Villa Parties you get two English girls to clean and cook. Free wine. *Contributed by Donald F. White*

✻

From the election manifesto of a white Parsee candidate in the Zanzibar election: 'My skin may be white but my heart is as black as yours.' *Contributed by M. Subramaniam*

✻

The honeymoon is over when the dog fetches the slippers and the wife does the barking. *Contributed by L. Winthrop*

✻

On the occasion of the first night of one of George Bernard Shaw's plays, the author sent two complimentary tickets to Sir Winston Churchill, commenting: 'Please bring a friend, if you have one.' Mr Churchill replied he regretted being unable to attend the first night but would like to go on the second night 'if there is one'. *Contributed by R. Cox*

Driving instructor to confused lady at the wheel: 'You still have a few minutes of your time left. Shall I show you how to fill in the accident forms?' *Contributed by R. Lyons*

❊

Equality of the sexes will be achieved when, on observing a bald-headed woman, a man is heard to remark: 'My, how distinguished she looks!' *Contributed by R. Barns*

❊

Golfer: 'Absolutely shocking round! I've never played so badly before.' Caddie: 'Oh? You have played before, then?' *M. Bell*

❊

Even a ginger ale at a night club makes you think you're seeing double when you look at the bill. *Contributed by John G. Hay*

❊

My dear, I didn't give your secret away, I only exchanged it for another one. *Contributed by W. G. Comer*

❊

Nostalgia is the realization that things weren't as unbearable as they seemed at the time. *Contributed by R. G. Hunt*

Lady customer: 'Does this lipstick come off easily?' Assistant: 'Not if you put up a fight!' *Contributed by L. Winthrop*

✳

Boss to secretary (looking at his watch during a long session of dictation): 'Good gracious, it's long past lunch hour. I'll just nip out and have a quick bite to eat while you type these.' *Contributed by Anna M. Kirwan*

✳

Absence of occupation is not rest. *Contributed by B. Sergeant*

✳

All marriages are happy. It's living together afterwards that causes all the trouble. *Contributed by Alan Webber*

✳

By the time winter ended I had very little spring. *Contributed by Miriam Eker*

✳

Ninety percent of the friction of daily life is caused by tone of voice. *Contributed by C. J. Fleetwood*

✳

Many a man doesn't know a woman is dynamite until he drops her. *H. Stephen*

The man who blows his own trumpet is usually a soloist. *Contributed by Philip Pine*

The most awkward age for girls is between teddy bears and wolves. *Contributed by W. A. Clarke*

Woman to her husband, as he surveys the mangled bumper: 'I'll tell you how it happened, but you've got to promise not to laugh!' *Contributed by Andrew Cross*

✳

There is little difference between people – only money. *Contributed by L. Harris*

The girl who burns the candle at both ends is content with an old flame by the time she's 40. *R. J. Miller*

❋

There are two kinds of people in the world: those who want to be something and those who want to do something. There is less competition among the second. *Contributed by David Alexander*

❋

An auctioneer is a dangerous man with whom to be on nodding acquaintance. *Contributed by B. Ward*

❋

Overheard in the House of Commons: 'How long as he been speaking?' 'About half an hour.' 'What's he talking about?' 'He hasn't said.' *Contributed by A. W. Urquhart*

❋

Alimony – bounty on the mutiny. *Contributed by I. M. Griffiths*

❋

The trouble with each generation is that it has not read the minutes of the last meeting. *Contributed by D. P. Anderson.*

An intimation – 'The flowers in the church will be distributed to those who are sick after the evening service.' *Contributed by M. Smith*

✳

If a stockbroker makes a killing you won't have to look far for the bird. *Contributed by Richard Austin*

✳

An American in Whitehall was overheard asking a policeman, 'Could you direct me to the ruins of Barbara Castle?' *Contributed by J. Webster*

✳

The definition of a marriage bureau is a male order house. *E. Donald*

✳

A thing is usually easier said than done, unless you have a stutter. *Contributed by John Trickett*

✳

Men are like physical pains: as long as they are there we can only think of them but often we must make an effort to remember them. *Contributed by Gabrielle Mejean*

Heard on a not very clear public address system at the airport: 'Will the gentleman who left his hearing aid on the seat of flight 642 please call at the information desk.' *Contributed by F. C. Pyke.*

❄

A smile is the shortest distance between two people. *Victor Borge/contributed by P. L. Leigh-Breese*

❄

The pill prevents inflation. *Contributed by Dr B. Weir*

❄

The biggest gambler of all time was Lady Godiva – she put all she had on one horse. *Bud Flanagan/contributed by Arthur J. Lewis, MP*

❄

When a man tells me he is killing time, I remind him that time is killing him. *Contributed by B. J. Hargreaves*

❄

Had nature foreseen the invention of motor vehicles it would have been the pedestrian who was supplied with spare parts. *Contributed by S. Miller*

As Fritz Kreisler and a friend were strolling in New York, they passed a fish shop where there were rows of protruding eyes and gaping mouths on the slab. 'Ah,' said Kreisler, 'that reminds me – I have a concert tonight!' *Contributed by Bill Boorne*

Hobo, in reply to allegations of stupidity: 'Many of us are very intelligent illiterates.' *Contributed by Alasdair Riley*

Talk to a man about himself and he will listen for hours. *Disraeli/contributed by C. J. Fleetwood*

❋

The trouble with life is that there are so many beautiful women and there is so little time. *Contributed by Dewi Lewis*

❋

When a boy was asked to state the greatest achievement of the Romans, he replied, 'Speaking Latin.' *Contributed by A. M. Jepson*

❋

The definition of a nun is a bird of pray. *W. Gillies*

❋

Love is the illusion that there is a difference between women. *Contributed by S. Leleux*

❋

Advertisement in the local press – Wanted to rent, house and buildings suitable for pigs. *Contributed by F. Hempsall*

❋

The feminine of a bachelor is a lady in waiting. *Contributed by B. Ward*

A gentleman is one who can borrow a pound with such charm as to make the lender feel ashamed he could not afford to offer a fiver. *Contributed by H. O'Malley*

✳

Farmer at a dinner: 'Why didn't you laugh at the Chairman's joke, everybody else did?' His friend: 'I never liked that fellow. I'll laugh when I get home.' *Contributed by E. F. Balloch*

✳

A philosopher may despise riches, but I'll bet his wife doesn't. *Contributed by Philip Pine*

✳

The poor have sometimes objected to being badly governed; the rich have always objected to being governed at all. *G. K. Chesterton/contributed by C. J. Fleetwood*

✳

Bigamy – when two rites make a wrong. *J. Johnson*

✳

The definition of a wig – an assumed mane. *R. Dorman*

✳

A Roman gladiator is an Atheist who lets his business mix with pleasure in a vicious circle. *Contributed by M. Duffy*

The art of taxation consists in so plucking the goose as to obtain the largest possible amount of feathers with the smallest possible amount of hissing. *Contributed by André Schuler*

❋

A sceptic is a man who won't take know for an answer. *G. James*

❋

Smart people don't break the law, they just bend it a little. *Contributed by Michael Hynes*

❋

Who you know is no longer enough, it's what you've got on who you know! *Contributed by Anna M. Kirwan*

❋

Nothing is impossible to the man who doesn't have to do it himself. *Contributed by W. A. Clarke*

❋

One consolation of being over 40 is that you can no longer die young. *Contributed by R. N. Hargrove*

❋

'I didn't come to be told I'm burning the candle at both ends,' said a patient to his doctor, 'I came for more wax.' *Contributed by M. Jennison*

Index of Contributors

✳

Burke, Billie, 58
Burman, I., 10
Bushman, M., 88
Button, Henry, 27
Byron, Lord, 55

Calhoun, E. E., 4
Cannon, Jimmy, 27
Canterbury, Terry, 54
Carr-Gregg, J. R., 62
Carroll, J., 99
Carroll, Lewis, 44
Carter, J., 42
Castle, N., 68
Ceder, Fay, 25
Chase, Evelyn, 41
Chase, I., 98
Chazel, 49
Clark, D., 100
Clark, D. M., 76, 85
Clark, Desmond, 81, 91, 105, 110, 112, 116
Clark, John, 91
Clarke, W. A., 93, 101, 104, 110, 115, 119, 122, 129
Clouston, George, 73
Clyde, B., 49
Coates, John E. H., 93
Cocteau, Jean, 17
Coe, M., 1
Cohen, Terry, 98
Collins, G., 87
Colliss, J. P., 23
Colyer, David, 37
Comer, W. G., 37, 41, 42, 59, 63, 82, 90, 95, 105, 112, 114, 120
Communication, 4, 11, 13, 14, 19, 59, 61
Conway, John, 55
Conway, S., 75
Cooke, J., 18
Cool, Norris, 6, 47
Cooper, John, 48
Cooper, Richard, 88

Courtney, H., 5
Cox, R., 119
Craig, E., 8
Cross, A. R., 75
Cross, Andrew, 45, 59, 68, 74, 83, 84, 89, 92, 95, 103, 114, 122
Cullis, F. A., 22
Curran, John Philpot, 77
Cuthbert, J. W., 92

Damone, Vic., 30
Daninds, Pierre, 54
Davidson, J., 29
Day, M., 6
Day, Simon, 32
Dayman, G. N., 64, 66, 73
Denny, Rupert, 15
Dible, J., 86, 101
Dickey, A., 31
Dirkman, E., 64, 73
Donald, E., 124
Donovan, Kevin, 110
Dorman, R., 128
Dorsey, Robert E., 38
Drinkall, John, 11, 13
Duffy, M., 128
Dumas, Alexandre, 41

Edbrook, A., 68
Eker, Miriam, 121
Elliott, Peter, 61
Ellis, Edmund, 111
Emerson, R. W., 44
Erskine, John, 108
Evans, Caradoc, 86
Evans, Peter, 15
Evening Standard, 8
Ewell, Tom, 3

Farmer, D., 81
Farmer, P. G., 15
Farre, Frank, 3
Fenn, Colin, 115
Field, Barnett, 103

[132]